IN UNCERTAINTY

How Shifting Your Mindset Transforms the Way You Live Life,
Pursue Purpose, and Thrive in Business

TRINETTA POWELL, LPC

Confidence in Uncertainty: How Shifting Your Mindset Transforms the Way You Live Life, Pursue Purpose, and Thrive in Business. Copyright © by Trinetta Powell.

All rights reserved. Printed in the United States of America.

No part of this book may be used or reproduced in any manner whatsoever without written permission except in the case of brief quotations embodied in critical articles and reviews. Scripture is taken from the New International Version of the Bible.

For information, address DW Creative Publishers, 5 Cowboys Way, Frisco, TX 75034.

DW Creative Publishers books may be purchased for business, educational, religious, or sales promotional use. For information, please email connect@dwcreativepublishers.com.

To connect with the author, Trinetta Powell, visit

www.ConfidenceInUncertainty.com.

FIRST EDITION

Cover design by: Trinetta Powell Consulting

Interior design by: DW Creative Publishers

Editing by: Leah Montgomery

PRINT BOOK: ISBN 978-1-952605-32-1

Library of Congress Control Number: 2023934276

CONTENTS

INTRODUCTION	1
PART 1: THRIVING IN MY LIFE	
THE BACKSTORY: SEE WHAT HAD HAPPENED WAS	5
THE ALMOST COLLEGE: DROP-OUT	9
PART 2: THRIVING IN BUSINESS	
THE 5 C'S TO SUCCESS	17
COURAGEOUS: TIME TO PUT ON YOUR BIG GIRL PANTIES	19
COMMITMENT: NO ONE CAN DO IT FOR YOU	25
COMMUNITY: IRON SHARPENS IRON	29
CLAIM IT: YOU GOTTA BELIEVE IT BEFORE YOU SEE IT	33
CONSISTENCY: NO ACTION, NO SUCCES	39
REFERENCES	41

INTRODUCTION

Let me take a minute and introduce myself. My name is Humpty, pronounced with an Umpty. Yo ladies, oh how I like to hump thee. And all the rappers in the top ten--please allow me to bump thee. I'm steppin' tall, y'all and just like Humpty Dumpty, you're gonna fall when the stereos pump me. Hey Y'all! I couldn't help myself. Thanks to Digital Underground or JAY-Z' Public Service Announcement every time I say let me introduce myself one of those songs automatically plays in my head. Just imagine me at speaking engagements trying not to bust out in the rap lyrics and doing the humpty dance when it's time to introduce myself. My teens and early adulthood is narrated by 90's Hip Hop. So, you may or may not see some references along the way in this book. Okay now let's get back on task. I am Trinetta Powell, Licensed Professional Counselor, Virtual Mental Health Practice Business Consultant, and Success Fulfillment Strategist. I am a wife, mom of 2 boys, bonus mom to 3 amazing peeps, sister, daughter, and Gigi to 7 grandbabies. And before you say it, yes, I'm too young to be Gigi, but God had other plans and they are a joy.

I am the owner of a multi-6 figure mental health private practice, able to give my kids a life of needs and many wants, and well on my way to hit the 7 figure mark by 2024. Now, it wasn't always this way. To be honest I haven't always been able to confidently out loud share and celebrate my wins and successes like that in the past. There was a time when I was a single mom struggling on welfare and food stamps, a nursing school drop-out, and questioned if I was ever going to make a better life for me and my oldest son. I found myself in many moments of depression and anxiety.

I have learned over the last 20 years some lessons and cultivated some skills that took me from living paycheck to paycheck to grossing multiple 6 figures a year and implementing a mindset for success in my business and personal life. I am writing this book because I want to share these lessons with you. I am a believer that your upbringing doesn't have to determine your future, that everyone has a birthright to achieve their dreams, and it's my responsibility to share my knowledge to make the path easier for the peeps coming behind and beside me. The vision you see in your head that you think is too far out of reach is possible and I am going to show you how in this book.

PART 1

THRIVING IN MY LIFE

THE BACKSTORY

SEE WHAT HAD HAPPENED WAS

You need to know where someone has been to appreciate and understand where they are now. I was born and raised in Mobile, AL, home of Mardi Gras, beaches, fresh seafood, and the best barbeque. I am the oldest child from my mother and the middle child from my daddy. I had an eventful childhood filled with love, laughter, and tons of family. But it also consisted of witnessing domestic violence in the home, drug abuse, and molestation. I grew up most of my life in subsidized housing or in neighborhoods where I wasn't allowed to walk down the street because they sold drugs there. I was known as the girl in middle school who never came outside and when I did come out, I didn't go any further than my front porch.

My grandparents were big influences in making sure we went to church every Sunday and participated in every church ministry possible for a kid. I was in the choir, usher board, Sunshine Crusaders, attended BTU and Vacation Bible School consistently. I'm sure God said why do y'all have this child in the choir, this is not the gift I gave her. I agreed, but if you are a part of a black church-going family then you know I had no choice in the matter. Some of my most fond memories as a child were at church. I made long lasting friends and had many parental influences that have guided me to adulthood. On the flip side there are parts of my childhood I wish I could forget.

I still can hear my mother's voice begging my father to not whip her with the belt when I was a kid. There were many nights I would cry myself to sleep listening to my parents argue and fight. When I was seven years old, I remember coming home from school and thought it was odd that my extended family was in our apartment. As I walked down the hall and entered my mother's room, I saw her lying in the bed with a broken jaw wired shut courtesy of my dad. This was the last straw and my dad moved out. He left me a note. I can't remember what it said, but I remember feeling broken, confused, and sad. I was sad that my dad was gone. I was sad my mom was hurting. The rest of my childhood was my dad being an inconsistent part of my life and not reliable. In my adulthood I took time to process my relationship with my dad. We will not see eye to eye on my perspective of my childhood; he was under the influence of drugs during that time and functioned how a parent would in that capacity. In the world of therapy, I decided to embrace a concept called Radical Acceptance towards his role as my dad. Radical Acceptance is accepting the situation/experience as it is. It's understanding that I can't change it and choosing to take my power back versus wishing things were different. Doing that gave me the courage to move forward and not allow my past to impact my future in a negative way. In other words, coming to terms and saying, "It is what it is".

I grew up in a single parent household with my mom. My mom was a hard worker, and she always made a way. Life was financially hard for her, but I wouldn't have known it. I always had everything I needed and a few things I wanted. I never felt like I was left out. Things began to change when she met my stepdad. My mom was excellent at giving love, supporting others even when they didn't deserve it, and extending grace. However, because of her past, she didn't always know how to trust or receive love. My stepdad was a man who was steady, cool, and calm. He was the balance my mom needed. This man was the most patient and kind person. He demonstrated unconditional love daily. He was the man who restored my mother's faith and trust in love. They gave me the best present in the world, my baby sister. I begged and asked for a sibling for the longest, and if you ask my mother, she said she wasn't really trying to make my wish come true. Nonetheless, I had a new best friend at 9 years old. My sister has been spoiled by me most of her life and I wouldn't change a second of it. I love being a big sister.

Fast forward a few years. My high school experience was great. I got my first job as cashier at Foot Locker on my 16th birthday, I was a flag girl in the marching band, and went to prom 3 years in a row! Despite all of that I still had doubts about who I was, if I would get into college, and struggled with confidence. Most of my friends were smarter than me. The Honor Society and Gifted program types. I was an average student doing my best. My parents always told me I could be anything I wanted to be. I heard these affirmations, but I wasn't always sure if I could really do it. This is a true lesson in the saying, "Your Network determines your Net Worth" because all my friends are super smart, it pushed me to try harder and do better. I saw them apply for college enrichment summer programs; I did the same. When they were completing applications and FAFSA senior year, I did too. Because of my circle, I went to college. My parents didn't go to college, so they were not knowledgeable of the process. They were encouraging and pushed me to seek the resources that could help. I became the first person in my family to graduate from college and earn a Master's Degree.

You may be wondering why I am telling you all this. It's because I want you to know that I didn't have this cookie cutter middle class life. I grew up poor, struggled with self-doubt, and despite all that, I made a success of my life. If I can do it, then you can do it.

THE ALMOST COLLEGE

DROP-OUT

I can remember it just like it was yesterday. I had just spent the last several weeks of spring semester of 2002 pledging a new line of illustrious women of Delta Sigma Theta Sorority Inc., to say I was exhausted is an understatement. I had finals the next week. I studied as best as I could being a single momma to a two-year-old and surviving off fumes at this point, but it wasn't enough. As I logged on to the computer to look at my final grades, I saw I had failed my Med Surg Course. I was devastated. Now to give you some background, I only had 2 more classes until I graduated with my Bachelor of Science in Nursing degree. Failing this course meant I would have to sit out for a year and reapply to complete the degree. There was no guarantee they would readmit me either. I was so disappointed in myself; I cried for days, prayed to God and pleaded for a solution. I had always dreamed of becoming a nurse and now that dream was being denied. I called all the other universities in my area to see if I could transfer to finish and they all said the same thing, "you would have to start the nursing program from the beginning." I was like nope, I ain't going through 2 years of nursing school all over again. God must have a different plan for me because this can't be it.

Once I got myself together, I began to ask myself now what? The thought of sitting out for a year and not getting accepted seemed like a waste of time. I prayed some more and asked God what I should do. He brought to my attention a comment from one of my Clinical professors. She said I was good at what I was doing but I spent too much time talking with the patients. That led to a realization how I enjoyed listening to people's stories and learning how they navigated life. I made a pivot and changed my major to Sociology and graduated with a BS after an 8-year college career.

Yes, you read that right, I said 8 years of college to get my BS degree y'all! When I counsel young adults and older adults who question if it's too late to start school or finish school after a long break, I tell them my story and remind them it's never too late to go after what you want. If you only knew the comments of, "how long you are going to be in school, she won't finish, and doesn't she know how hard it's going to be to finish college with a baby." The noise from outsiders and some family would play in the back of my mind at times. I used their perceptions of me as fuel to push forward and acknowledge that a pivot is not a set-back. I went on to get my Master's Degree in Counseling as well. I was the first in my family to earn a graduate degree. Receiving my graduate degree with my husband and kids watching was one of the highlights of my life.

Here is what I learned in those years of undergrad and grad school, the perception of myself is greater than the perception others have of me. I spent too much time worrying about what others thought of me in my twenties. The moment I learned to focus on what I thought of myself and what I was capable of with God at the center was the game changer. My perception of me is what sustains my momentum in the hard times. Thank ya sweet baby Jesus for deliverance of people pleasing!

Why Am I Stuck

If I had a dime for how many times my clients say, "I feel stuck", I would already be a millionaire. Feeling stuck can feel like you are not in alignment with your purpose. You know your current situation is not what you want it to be, and too afraid to go after what you think you should be doing. Fear is the glue that keeps you stuck. Fear is defined as being afraid of someone or something that can be dangerous, threatening, or painful. For me my fear was being afraid of failure, letting my family down, and shame in the possibility of proving the naysayers right. I am a recovering victim of impostor syndrome. I say recovering because it never goes away completely but I have learned to keep it in check. We will talk about how later in the book. Impostor syndrome is when you believe you are not capable of accomplishing a goal, lack confidence in your abilities, or possibly believe you are not worthy of success. I allowed imposter syndrome to keep me from advancing my career and waited 7 years to take my National Counselors Exam to become a Licensed Therapist. This was 7 years living in a space of doubting myself, believing that working a state job was stability because that's what I was taught, and convincing myself I didn't have the finances to waste on a test I wouldn't pass. My mindset was a hot mess. This was not my first experience with imposter syndrome, I can remember as early as middle and high school believing I was not as smart as my friends. Mine you I was attending the same Preparatory School and Magnet High School and in some of the same classes; yet I still believed they were better. I was just as smart but didn't believe it despite us walking the same path.

Sometime around my early 30's there was a shift in my mindset. I entered a space of wanting more. In 2010, I took the leap and moved with my husband and 2 boys 10 hours away from my mom, siblings and extended family. We had no family support in Texas. My husband and I were going to sink or swim. Everyone thought we were crazy. At this time, we both had been laid off from our jobs within 2 weeks of each other. It was a year after the Great Recession and jobs were not so abundant in our city. The mortgage was still due every month on the first, so we took a chance on faith and headed to Dallas. I totally believe with all my heart that moving to Texas and being in an environment that offered so much more opportunity than my hometown sparked something in me. I wanted to break generational chains of robbing Peter to pay Paul and wanted to provide for my kids in ways my parents never could but wanted. In order to do this Faith had to be activated to break those chains and build generational wealth.

I started digging deep in my Faith that God will fill in the gaps. I hung on tight to the writings in James 2:14-26 in the Bible. Most are familiar with a portion of the scripture that says Faith without works is dead. The text goes on to say, someone may say, "You have faith, and I do things. Prove to me you have faith when you are doing nothing. I will prove to you I have faith by doing things." This is true, you can't have one without the other. I told myself if I do the work by studying for the National Counselors Exam and believe God would grant me favor then His Will would be done. I took the test and passed on the first try! I felt overwhelmed with gratitude and excitement. This gave me so much confidence in myself and relief that I don't have to do any of this alone. It also reminded me that I have help, God wants me to win, and affirmed my belief I was on track doing what God had called me to do. It gave me the push I needed to keep going. The more I trusted God and did the work the more my life felt aligned with purpose.

Your purpose is tied to the breakthrough of others in the world. Our gifts and talents are meant to serve the community. If we don't show up, we could be delaying someone else's journey to purpose, deliverance, or healing.

PART 2

THRIVING IN BUSINESS

THE 5 C'S TO SUCCESS

In my journey in entrepreneurship, I learned there were a few key elements needed for me to be successful. Just saying I will stay motivated, and I won't quit until I reach my goal wasn't enough. I didn't understand the How to stay motivated and to not quit in the beginning. Through self-exploration and evaluation of the steps I took when I was successful and what environment sustained it led to what I call the 5 C's to Success. They are Courageous, Commitment, Community, Claim It, and Consistency. We will explore these elements in Part 2 of this book.

COURAGEOUS

TIME TO PUT ON YOUR BIG GIRL PANTIES

Dorothy Bernard:

"Courage is fear that has said its prayers."

Vulnerability takes courage and being courageous takes vulnerability. You can't have one without the other. We can easily criticize ourselves by picking out all the things we don't do well but struggle to identify the things we can do well or great. The idea of putting my true self and desires for my life out in the open was too scary. Like most people I feared rejection and was anxious about what people would think, and how they would judge me. Through my training as a Licensed Professional Counselor and going through the process of therapy on my own I have learned that vulnerability is a superpower.

Brene` Brown is a research professor who has been studying vulnerability, courage, shame, and empathy for over 20 years. She went viral for her TEDx Houston talk on vulnerability in 2010. She has written several books on these topics, and I find her work insightful in my journey to be confident and bold in my life. Brene` says vulnerability is about investigating and accepting imperfection, understanding that doing so will piss some people off, and having the willingness to accept criticism and own your mistakes. For me as a black woman who was raised in the South, there were certain standards and expectations in my family. I was taught to be seen and not heard, repeatedly told I am a reflection of my family when I walk out the door and to always be on my best behavior. You know the famous line black moms say, "You better not embarrass me". I mean, I was for the most part an obedient child growing up, minus the teenage years when my older sister influenced my poor decision making. I mean everyone borrows their grandma's car and sneaks out of the house with their younger sister, right? I know I'm not the only one but that's another story for another book. I don't know if that could be considered courage or just plain old young and dumb, lol. But seriously, after studying Brene's work on shame, vulnerability, and empathy, I have learned these messages in my upbringing influenced my feelings of shame and resistance to vulnerability.

When I went off to college, I had 3 roommates. One day we were getting ready to go out to check out a campus event and I was ironing my t-shirt. Now this was a basic t-shirt I think with the college logo on it. My roommate thought it was crazy to be ironing a cotton t-shirt. I told her my momma and grandmother would have a fit if I left that dorm in a wrinkled shirt. My mindset was I had to be presentable when going out in public because I was a representation of my upbringing. At this time this was a pattern of giving others perception of me/my family too much power in how I lived my life. In this example it was a t-shirt, but on several occasions, it spilled over into money mindset, parenting choices, and spirituality. The idea of putting my true self and desires for my life out in the open was too scary. When I would try to step outside of the box, I would sabotage myself by over analyzing it. I wanted to be seen as perfect. The one who represented her family well. I was the one who was afraid to cheat on a test or skip class in high school because my mother was not going for it. That perfectionism takes a toll over time.

Perfectionism can be seen by some people as a positive trait that encourages high achievement that equates to success. However, it can be the exact opposite. Perfectionism disguises itself as a positive strategy to success when in reality it creates a narrative of false identity. I call it the birthplace of impostor syndrome. Another profound way to look at perfectionism described by Brene` Brown is, "When Perfectionism is driving, shame is always riding shotgun and Fear is the annoying backseat driver. Perfectionism is believing if I look perfect, live perfect, and work perfect, I can avoid criticism, blame and ridicule. This Perfectionism keeps us from being seen. The way to get out of the mindset of perfectionism is healthy striving."

I was working with a client who was the go-to for everyone in her family. She was the problem solver, the rescuer, the financial support, and the peacemaker. She was a third parent to her sibling, first to graduate college, and made a comfortable life for herself. She was making 6 figures, miserable in her job, and felt pressure to be perfect to make sure her family was proud of her. Because she placed her value in the hands of her family, it led to anxiety, not feeling her needs were important, and resentment was built. I worked with her to learn to set boundaries, gain confidence in putting herself first, and understand in doing all this she was going to make others mad and that's okay.

The only perfect person is Jesus. No matter how hard you try, you can't be him nor should you want to be. The mind is funny though, even though we cognitively can understand the concept that no one is perfect, we still tell ourselves we must try. This mind can be a hindrance sometimes, whew!

In February 2020 I was courageous and decided to launch my private practice not knowing the pandemic would be hitting a month later. To say starting my business was overwhelming was an understatement. There was so much I didn't know, like who to trust for help, then feeling discouraged when I did ask and people flaked; I was afraid to make decisions for fear of messing up. I was in a state of analysis paralysis. Analysis Paralysis is the state of over analyzing the situation or decision that needs to be made so much that no action is taken. This is a type of self-sabotage that can lead to procrastination, stress, anxiety, and depression.

If you find you struggle with Perfectionism as well, here are a few mindset shifts I have learned in my training and have implemented in my own life: See yourself from a perspective that is balanced with both strengths and weaknesses versus seeing only the extremes as either perfect or a failure. Secondly, set standards that are achievable but challenging, and feel content when they are met versus setting impossible standards for success and feeling upset when they are not met. The 3rd shift is being motivated by the potential of success and happiness versus being motivated by fear of failure, criticism, or rejection. This last mindset shift was the most impactful for me as it helped me reach my goal of operating a muli-6 figure business in less than 2 years.

COMMITMENT

NO ONE CAN DO IT FOR YOU

Isaiah 45:2

I will go before thee, and make the crooked path straight: I will break in pieces the gates of brass, and cut in sunder the bars of iron.

At the start of the year many Americans make New Year resolutions or set goals they want to accomplish by December 31st. The University of Scranton conducted a study and found that only 8% of people will achieve their New Year's resolutions. Studies have shown that 80% of people fail to achieve their resolutions despite efforts to approach them differently according to forbes.com. Committing to our goals has consistently been proven to be tough. So how does one become successful and strive to be in the 8%? Keep reading and I will tell you how to make it happen.

Commitment is having the courage to change. It's saying yes repeatedly when it gets boring, hard, or discouraging. When I made the decision to quit my 9-5 state job with great benefits and flexibility, I had to have commitment to the decision. My family needed my income along with my husband's to support us. I couldn't half-step on this one. I announced to my co-workers in May 2020 that by the end of the year I will no longer be a w-2 employee. I don't think they believed me fully. I had moments of my own when me and Jesus had some real heart to hearts on this decision. I was scared but I was willing to do it anyway. I have learned that when I'm doing something that seems so big that it scares me, I know I need Jesus to pull it off. In these experiences is when I am blessed the most and God gets all the glory.

Making the decision to quit my job for entrepreneurship was the easiest part of the commitment process. How I was going to earn the 60k to replace my salary was a whole nother story. The action and consistency it took to make it happen was the hard part. I calculated how many clients I needed to see per week in my practice to equal a salary of 60k per year and I needed to save 3 months of cushion to cover household expenses. I needed to see 15 clients a week on top of working my 9-5 and save 15k. Talk about heart pounding and anxiety thinking about all the what ifs. But I was committed because I was clear on my why.

Around the time when I made the decision to quit my job my 19 year old son was facing a health crisis. It required me to miss a lot of work. We were frequent flyers of the emergency room, too many EGD's to count, and doctor follow up visits from the EGD's and hospital stays. The doctors' diagnosis required a potential liver transplant as his option for a cure, his medical bills were climbing, and we may have to support him financially for the rest of his life. I knew that my current job wouldn't be able to sustain the potential financial responsibilities I was facing. I wanted the freedom to be a caregiver to my son without worrying about meeting the demands of an employer. This was my push for taking the leap to leave my job. Now that I was clear on my why, it was time to start making things happen.

Launching a business was not in my zone of genius. I needed help on getting started to launch my practice. I had no clue where to begin. I knew the basics; get an LLC, EIN, and a website. I didn't know how to do all those things. This is the point where most just stop and say this is too hard and overwhelming. Truth is, it is intensely overwhelming to be in the land of the unknown. A lesson I had to learn quickly was, I can't possibly know how to do it all and I needed to ask for help. Like momma said, a closed mouth doesn't get fed. I have spent thousands on consultants, coaches, masterclass, and webinars learning skills to run my business. I have read books or shall I say listen to them on my Audible app to learn about business strategies and mindset work. I have a few of my favorites listed on my website www.trinettapowellconsulting.com in the resource section if you're interested.

I can remember in the early phase, I would work my 9-5, leave to see counseling clients in my solo practice, and spend my free nights and weekends building my website. The learning curve was so steep. The valley was not cool at all. I clung to scriptures like, "Ye though I walk through the valley and the shadow of death, I am with you; I can do all things through Christ that strengthen me; don't worry about anything, instead pray about everything." I knew I wasn't in this darkness alone and that gave me hope.

In order to remain committed keep saying yes, even when it looks like hell, because the light is just around the bend. Understand that you must invest in yourself. Your skills need to be sharpened. Just because you want to be an inspirational speaker, doesn't mean you know the framework and technique it takes to be a great speaker. Sharpening your skills could be taking a class, hiring a coach or mentor, reading a book, or paying to pick a consultant's brain. Not everything will be free, and believe you are worth the investment.

Destiny's Child

I'm a survivor
I'm not gon' give up
I'm not gon' stop
I'm gon' work harder
I'm a survivor
I'm gonna make it
I will survive
Keep on survivin'

COMMUNITY

IRON SHARPENS IRON

Ecclesiastes 4:9:10

Two are better than one, because they have a good return for their labor: If either of them falls down, one can help the other up.

Community has been an important part of my success in life. I know you've heard the quote "Your Network Determines Your Net worth". I can confidently say that this has been true for me. It was being in a group of friends in high school who strived for academic excellence that pushed me to do the same, and my current business besties that keep me motivated and sane now. Women supporting women has an impact that can expand across the world. Growing up I had a soundtrack of R&B/Rap songs that influenced the importance and impact of having great friends. Some of my favorites were TLC's "What About Your Friends", "Where My

Girls At" by 702, "Exhale" by the great Whitney Houston, and let's not forget Queen Latifah's "U.N.I.T.Y. " Here are a few things I've learned about being in a community.

Community cultivates **inspiration**. Being in an environment where I could see other women winning at life, in their business, or career was hope that I could do the same. When you are going after something that is hard, out of your comfort zone, and requires Jesus to pull it off you need inspiration. When I was in the process of making the decision to quit my job in 2020 to go full time in my business, I was SCARED. I needed to see other people doing it. I needed to watch them fail and recover better than before, I needed to be in a space where people understood what I would be facing, and they knew how to support me. Family and friends can't always be that for you. They won't understand what you are doing. They may even try to convince you to quit, not because they want to see you fail, but they may have never succeeded to the level you are trying to get to. They don't have to understand it, but you have to know when and what to share with whom and stay the course. You will fail, and you will succeed with help.

My business bestie Sharhonda holds me accountable, and I do the same for her. We connect daily via text, Facetime, or Marco Polo to report daily goals and a recap of what was done. We call each other out when we are allowing impostor syndrome to crept in, and gas each other up when making big leaps in business. Like the bible says "as iron sharpens iron, so one person sharpens another," Proverbs 27:17.

The second lesson I have learned is that I will not know everything. I have gained so much **knowledge** that has been valuable to me in this journey. The business masterminds and cohorts I have been part of have exposed me to knowledge I wouldn't have gotten on my own. There is most always someone available who can fill in a gap for you. Which led to my next lesson learned, **Connections**.

Having the opportunity to connect with other talented people gave me new perspectives in my approach with decision making. Sometimes, when we are hyper focused on a goal we can get tunnel vision. It helps to have an outside person give you their feedback from their lens to pull you out when you are stuck. Connecting with people whose gifts are different from yours can elevate your growth. I am a natural encourager, cheerleader, glass always half full person. I am not a salesperson, marketer, or tech savvy. Having connections with creatives to tech peeps help me grow my business.

Another benefit to community is **resources.** Being an entrepreneur, I had several learning curves and needed a lot of resources. I had communities focused on business foundations needs and others focused on clinical private practice needs. So, you may need different communities depending on where you need support. Being in community groups saved me from a lot of frustration by providing resources to solve my problems.

If you are not a part of a community, you should go find one today. I find my groups on Facebook. I am a part of black mom groups, black therapists groups, and private practice groups just to name a few. When faced with a challenge, being in a community will relieve the stress of the "What ifs" and "How am I going to do this?" It will evoke resilience that is necessary for success.

Jay Z

They trying to get they ones, I'm tryin' to get them M's
One million, two million, three million, four
In just five years, forty million more
You are now looking at the forty million boy
I'm rapping Def Jam 'til I'm the hundred million man -

CLAIM IT

YOU GOTTA BELIEVE IT BEFORE YOU SEE IT

Proverbs 23:7

For as he thinks within himself, so he is.

We can't predict the future, but God can and knows every detail of your journey. Michael Todd is the pastor of Transformation Church in Tulsa, Oklahoma. Last Fall he rebooted his Crazy Faith series where he talked about how we as Christians must have crazy faith to believe it before we see it. We must believe that the thing we are asking God for will happen before it actually happens. God calls us all to a purpose in life. I believe our first purpose is to expand God's kingdom by bringing more people to Christ and a by-product of doing that is through the gifts and talents God gives us.

As I evaluate my life and how successful I have been, I can say at the core of it all was my FAITH. When I consult with God before making a decision, he has always been faithful in his promises. The bible defines faith as the assurance of things hoped for, the conviction of things not seen. I believed I could move to Texas away from all family support and it was going to be okay. When I quit my second state job(I've had 3, lol) with great benefits with no job lined up, I knew I was going to be okay, and I had the same faith when I launched my business in 2020.

Mindset is everything. I teach my clients the cycle between our thoughts, behavior, and feelings. Our thoughts create feelings. Our feelings create behaviors. Our behavior reinforces thoughts. In life this could look like: you think you are not good enough, which makes you feel bad/sad about yourself, so you avoid engaging in relationships/going after a goal/career advancement. For example, you believe you are not skillful enough for a new position at work, which may make feel you are not smart therefore, won't apply for the job/promotion. This is what we would call a negative mindset. A negative mindset will cause you to remain stagnant in many areas of your life. It can lead to depression, low self-esteem, reduce your confidence, and can cause illness in the body.

A positive mindset would look like: I believe I can go back to school; I'm nervous and excited; I call the school to meet with an advisor. Having a positive mindset is making a conscious effort to check the negative thoughts and redirect them. Remaining in a positive mindset increases your motivation, confidence, chances of success, and life span.

While writing this book my faith was put to the test. I had an opportunity to pitch to this big New York City investment firm for a

$10,000 grant for my business. I had been working with their team of interns to solve a marketing issue. We had to pitch our problem, our solution, and how it impacted my business. They flew me out first class and paid for all my experiences. Side note, when you fly first class, you never want to go back to coach. As I sat in my seat, I took a minute to visualize myself with my family sitting first class for our next vacation, and I believe that it's going to happen.

When it came to the day of the pitch, I was more nervous and anxious than usual. I normally get a little nervous before speaking, but this felt different. I decided to put on Jireh by Elevation Church and Maverick City Music and let the words wash over me. As I worshipped, I felt a sense of calm come over me. I got dressed and headed to the office for rehearsals. As I listened to the other contestants talk about how nervous they were about their presentations, mixed with not meeting with my team yet, and all the instructions of where to go and to stand; I quickly became overwhelmed. I was out of my comfort zone. I had knots in my stomach, my breath started to quicken, and felt like I was headed to a panic attack.

I stopped, did some box breathing, and took a walk. While walking I prayed to God that I wanted to win, for him to blow my mind today, and to let His Will be done. I went on to rehearse with my team and got into My Zone. After a few run throughs I felt great about my presentation.

Before the pitch, all the contestants presented display tables for guests and judges to see our products and ask questions. The other contestants had beautiful displays of the products they sold. I had no real physical products to place on a table besides the new marketing brochure my team designed. Not having anything physical to show made me feel insecure and question my importance among the group. That insecurity triggered my negative thinking of shame, perfectionism, and feeling not good enough. I told myself to stay focus and hold on to my little piece of faith of believing my work is valid and worthy of being recognized. Very few people stopped by to talk to me, but the few that did were very engaged and interested in my mission to serve Black Indigenous People of Color (BIPOC) heal from anxiety, depression, and trauma. When the time came to do our pitch, everything went great. I sat and listened to the other six teams pitch, and every time doubt began to creep in my mind as I compared their presentation to ours in my head. I redirected my thoughts by silently praying, Lord Let Your Will Be Done. It was time for the vote and my business name was spelled wrong on the ballot. I was like God really; people were going to be confused. My team was upset with the mistake. An announcement was made to let voters know that Refill should say Reveal. I again said silently, Lord Let Your Will Be Done. They called us back for the announcement of the winner, and again I said, Lord Let Your Will Be Done as I held my breathe. It was like the room went silent as they said the winner is Reveal and Restore. I had a millisecond delayed reaction before I screamed. Ya'll, we had won! I couldn't believe it. My team was excited as well, and we took a ton of pictures and celebrated afterwards.

I had gone in an environment that looked like I was set up for failure and God blessed me. Stepping into a space that felt like it may be impossible for me to achieve the goal I was going after revealed some takeaways for the next time I am faced with this same challenge in the future.

1. Make my request known to God

2. Call on my community of support for prayers in the preparation and execution period
3. Having Faith, the size of a mustard seed is enough
4. A scarcity mindset is not a mindset of abundance and God's will for my life
5. Do it scared
6. I'm worth taking a chance on
7. Continue to show up as my authentic self and be seen
8. Every time I step into an uncomfortable situation and come out on the other side victorious, my confidence grows.

Elevation Church and
Maverick City Music

Jireh, You are enough
Jireh, You are enough

I will be content in every circumstance
Jireh, You are enough

CONSISTENCY

NO ACTION, NO SUCCESS

Galatians 6:9

And let us not grow weary of doing good, for in due season we will reap, if we do not give up.

There are times when I want to say forget it all and run off to some tropical island away from all the decisions, responsibilities, and frustrations of business and family. I never would quit on myself or my family, but I had to learn an easier way to manage my home and reach my goals. When you are faced with a big transition or starting the process of making a change in your life you have to first know the difference between a goal and a habit. Goals are outcomes and habits are the actions you take to achieve a goal. My goal was to quit my 9-5. It was the habits that helped me to have a successful business. For me, creating a habit plan fostered gaining momentum in my commitment by making small changes first and moving on to another change once I mastered that habit. I was working with a client and explaining this strategy to her. She wanted to work on multiple changes at once as she has done previously. Her perception was that it would take too long to accomplish her goals focusing on one habit at a time. I presented this to her. If you focus on one habit to master per month to achieve a goal, you could potentially achieve 12 goals in a year, or you can focus on multiple habits, as you have done in the past, with minimal to no results in goals achieved. She saw the light and agreed to go with the odds of joining the 8% of Americans who meet their goals.

I have had to develop habits in my business for it to be successful. I tripled my gross income in my second year of business. That happened with a consistent routine and habits in place. Now it wasn't always easy. There were nights and days when I wanted to just throw the business in the trash, lol. Entrepreneurship is an emotional rollercoaster. On the rough days I would have to call on Jesus more and play some Mary J Blige or Frankie Beverly to get me through a project. No matter how frustrated I would get, I had to keep pushing forward with the next step I could see to take. Most people stop when they can't see the whole picture. I was one of those people. I had to learn that it's okay to not see the entire plan before moving forward. God will show me just what I need to see at the time. If he had shown me running my own business, I would have laughed. I was always the team player, and never saw myself as a boss. God took me through some storms of development in my work and personal life that prepared me for leadership. 100% of the time when it gets to be the hardest, the breakthrough is near. That's when you must dig deep in your faith and continue to do the work. Stay consistent on your path, it will be worth it.

REFERENCES

https://www.forbes.com/sites/kathycaprino/2019/12/21/the-top-3-reasons-new-years-resolutions-fail-and-how-yours-can-succeed/?sh=1a732c066992

https://www.forbes.com/sites/tracybrower/2021/12/31/4-reasons-to-make-new-years-resolutions-even-if-you-dont-keep-them/?sh=304cad9166a1

www.ingramcontent.com/pod-product-compliance
Lightning Source LLC
Chambersburg PA
CBHW042113120526
44592CB00042B/2792